The Effortless Investor

SRIRAM SARAVANAN

Dedication

To my Parents, Wife and Friends

Disclaimer

The information provided in this book "The Effortless Investor," is for educational and informational purposes only. It is intended to provide a general understanding of investment principles and strategies and should not be considered financial advice. The author and publisher make no representations or warranties of any kind, express or implied, about the completeness, accuracy, reliability, suitability, or availability with respect to the information, products, services, or related graphics contained in this book for any purpose. Any reliance you place on such information is therefore strictly at your own risk.

No Financial Advice

This book does not provide financial advice. The author is not a registered financial advisor, and the information contained herein should not be construed as such. The content of this book is not intended to be a substitute for professional financial advice from a qualified advisor who is aware of your individual financial situation. Always consult with a qualified financial advisor before making any investment decisions.

Investment Risks

Investing in financial markets involves risk, and past performance is not indicative of future results. The value of investments can go down as well as up, and you may lose some or all of your initial investment. The strategies and investments discussed in this book may not be suitable for all investors. It is your responsibility to understand the risks associated with any investment and to determine whether it is appropriate for your individual circumstances.

Specific Companies and Securities

Any references to specific companies, stocks, ETFs, or other securities are for illustrative purposes only. The mention of any specific security does not constitute a recommendation to buy, sell, or hold that security. The author and publisher do not endorse or promote any specific companies or securities mentioned in this book. The author and publisher are not responsible for the performance of any securities mentioned in this book.

Accuracy of Information

The information in this book is based on the author's understanding of financial markets and available information at the time of writing. While the author and publisher have made every effort to ensure the accuracy of the information contained in this book, they do not guarantee its accuracy, completeness, or timeliness. Financial markets are constantly changing, and the information in this book may become outdated.

Limitation of Liability

In no event will the author or publisher be liable for any loss or damage, including without limitation, indirect or consequential loss or damage, or any loss or damage whatsoever arising from loss of data or profits arising out of, or in connection with, the use of this book

Reader Responsibility

The reader is solely responsible for their own investment decisions. By reading this book, you acknowledge that you have read, understood, and agreed to this disclaimer. You agree to hold harmless the author and publisher from any and all claims, losses, or damages arising from your use of the information in this book.

External Links

From time to time, this book may contain links to other websites. These links are provided for your convenience to provide further information. They do not signify that the author or publisher endorse the website(s). The author and publisher have no responsibility for the content of the linked website(s).

No Assurance of Results

The author and publisher make no assurance or guarantee that the use of the information in this book will lead to profitable investments or financial success.

Professional Advice

This book is not a substitute for professional financial, legal, or tax advice. Consult with a qualified professional for advice tailored to your specific situation.

INTRODUCTION

The Phone Rings...

The insistent ring of my phone shattered the afternoon calm. Glancing at the screen, I saw it was Michael, a friend I often called Mr. Shortcut – a nickname that reflected his fast-paced approach to life, including his finances. I'd occasionally discussed investing with him, and I'd always encouraged him to take a long-term, strategic approach. But lately, he'd been uncharacteristically quiet on that front.

Picking up the phone, I braced myself for whatever news Michael had. His voice on the other end was a stark contrast to his usual chipper self – strained, barely a whisper.

"*Sriram,*" he croaked, "*I lost it all.*"

My stomach lurched. A wave of dread washed over me. A few weeks prior, we'd spent a casual evening at a bar, catching up. As always, the conversation eventually turned to investing. I patiently explained the virtues of long-term investing, the power of compounding interest, and how a steady approach could turn even a modest portfolio into a wealth-generating machine.

I even introduced him to the concept of Exchange-Traded Funds (ETFs) – these remarkable investment vehicles I'd get into more detail later.

Michael seemed receptive, even taking copious notes on a bar napkin. I left that night feeling optimistic, hopeful that he was finally embracing a smarter approach to building wealth. But this phone call... this was different.

"*What do you mean you lost it all?*" I asked, my voice trembling slightly.

A long, defeated sigh escaped the other end of the line. "*Remember that hot stock I was asking you about? The one that was supposed to double my money in a month?*" His voice cracked. "*Well... it didn't.*"

Dread turned to a cold certainty. Michael hadn't heeded my warnings about chasing quick riches. He'd ignored the patient, long-term strategy I'd outlined and instead plunged headfirst into the risky world of day trading individual stocks. And as often happens in such cases, the market had delivered a harsh lesson.

That evening, we met again at the same bar – a somber reunion compared to our previous, optimistic gathering. Beers were ordered, but the atmosphere was heavy with regret.

This time, there was no enthusiastic note-taking, no animated discussions about the latest investment trends. Just a palpable sense of defeat hanging in the air.

I started with the basics, easing him back into the world of investing, but this time from a different angle. I talked about the importance of patience, the power of diversification, and how even the most seasoned investors understand that trying to beat the market consistently is a near-impossible feat.

Then came the question, no longer fueled by a desire for quick gains, but by a desperate hope for recovery.

"*So*," he said, his voice barely a whisper,"*is there anything I can do to get back on track? Is there some kind of investment that can help me recover from this?*"

I took a deep breath. "*Listen closely, Michael*," I said, leaning in conspiratorially. "*Most people go broke chasing that one hot stock or magical formula. You won't get rich quick, but if you're truly serious about building wealth for the long term, there is a way. And it's not just any ordinary investment.*"

His eyes, previously clouded with disappointment, flickered with a spark of curiosity.

"*There's a special kind of investment,*" I continued, lowering my voice for dramatic effect, "*that's like holding a basket of the entire global economy in your portfolio. Imagine owning a piece of thousands of companies, all rolled into one. It won't erase your losses overnight, but it can put you on a path to steady, stress-free growth over the long term. It's called an Exchange Traded Fund, or ETF. Think of it as an umbrella under which multiple stocks are held. And there's one ETF in particular that's not just any ETF. It's like an ETF of ETFs.*"

"*Wow,*" he breathed, captivated by the idea. "*What is it called?*"

I took a sip of my beer, savoring the moment. "*You'll find out later in the book*" I said with a wink.

Yes, dear reader, I just broke the fourth wall — *like Deadpool, but with ETFs.*

Consider it the ultimate cliffhanger, like waiting for the next season of your favorite show. Trust me, the wait will be worth it.

This book, my dear reader, is definitely not for people who chase get-rich-quick schemes, only to end up back where they started.

It's for those who are tired of the constant rollercoaster ride of individual stocks and are ready to invest for the long term, with a smarter, more strategic approach.

Within these pages, you won't find a magical stock pick or a "get rich quick" scheme. What you will find is a clear and actionable roadmap – a proven strategy to build wealth slowly, consistently, and stress-free. I'll equip you with the knowledge to understand why this approach works, and then I'll finally reveal the ETF I've been hinting at — among others.

Are you ready to ditch the stress and become an "*Effortless Investor*"?

Let's get started!

Some Stats before we begin...

Here's the thing about investing: there's this huge idea out there that the "*experts*" – the fund managers who charge big fees – are the ones who can really make you money. They're supposed to have some special skill, right?

Well, get this...

For over 20 years, S&P Dow Jones Indices (*these guys are the authority on this stuff*) has been tracking how these "*experts*" actually perform. They put together these reports called the SPIVA scorecard, and it's basically a head-to-head comparison between the pros and, well, just investing in the overall market (like the *S&P* 500).

And the results? They're jaw-dropping. Seriously.

- Most "experts" don't beat the market: The SPIVA data consistently shows that most of those actively managed funds – the ones with the high fees and the fancy talk – fail to outperform. And we're not talking about just a bad year here and there.
- It gets worse over time: What's even crazier is that the longer you look, the harder it is for these "experts" to keep up. Beating the market in the long run? Apparently, it's incredibly difficult.

Let me give you a mind-blowing example.

The SPIVA U.S. Year-End 2023 report found that over the past 20 years, a massive 83% of active large-cap funds couldn't even keep pace with the S&P 500.

Think about that for a second.

What does this mean?

It's not about whether active management could work in some perfect world. It's about what the data consistently tells us about how it works in the real world.

And the SPIVA data punches a big hole in the idea that paying those high fees for "*expert*" management actually gets you better results.

That's the core idea behind "*The Effortless Investor*."

It's about a simple, proven way to invest that doesn't depend on finding these mythical "*experts*."

Source: S&P Dow Jones Indices, SPIVA U.S. Year-End 2023.

Want to see the data for yourself? You can find the full SPIVA reports here:

- https://www.spglobal.com/spdji/en/research-insights/spiva/

CHAPTER 1

Your First $10,000:

Making Smart ETF Choices

The allure of striking it rich by picking the "next big thing" is a powerful siren song for many investors. We've all heard the stories – that one friend-of-a-friend who invested in a small startup that went on to become a tech giant, turning their modest investment into a life-changing fortune.

These tales fuel the dream of uncovering the hidden gem, the undiscovered stock that will skyrocket in value, making us wealthy beyond our wildest imaginations.

But these stories, while inspiring, often obscure a harsh reality: consistently picking winning stocks is incredibly difficult, even for seasoned professionals.

In fact, the vast majority of actively managed funds, run by highly educated, experienced and the Wall Street's finest, fail to beat the performance of simple market indexes over the long term.

The following tables illustrates the persistent underperformance of these "experts" / actively managed funds across some major markets such as the U.S., Canada, Europe and Australia, over various time horizons:

Time Period	% of Active Funds Underperforming the Index (USA)
1 Year	57%
3 Years	86%
5 Years	77%
10 Years	85%

Time Period	% of Active Funds Underperforming the Index (Canada)
1 Year	80%
3 Years	76%
5 Years	89%
10 Years	93%

Time Period	% of Active Funds Underperforming the Index (Europe)
1 Year	84%
3 Years	94%
5 Years	91%
10 Years	92%

Time Period	% of Active Funds Underperforming the Index (Australia)
1 Year	65%
3 Years	70%
5 Years	68%
10 Years	82%

Source: S&P Dow Jones Indices SPIVA Report

As this table starkly illustrates, the challenge of outperforming the market isn't confined to the US. Even in Canada, Australia, and Europe, the vast majority of active fund managers across various categories struggle to beat their respective benchmarks over the long term.

This phenomenon is often referred to as the "winner's curse" – the idea that the stock that appears most promising is often already overvalued, priced for perfection, leaving little room for further gains. So, if even Wall Street's finest struggle to consistently outperform the market, what chance do individual investors have?

The answer, as we'll explore in this book, lies in a smarter, more strategic approach: investing in the whole market, not just individual stocks.

And the best part? You can achieve this outperformance effortlessly.

To understand this concept, let's journey to the fictional nation of Economia, where the snack food market is a fiercely competitive arena.

Three titans – Crunchy Chips, Zesty Crackers, and Sweet Biscuits – dominate the landscape, controlling a staggering 94% of all snack sales.

Each company boasts a loyal following, innovative products, and compelling marketing campaigns. For investors, this concentrated market presents a tempting, yet complex, dilemma.

Crunchy Chips, the upstart challenger, has captured the hearts (and taste buds) of the younger generation with its bold flavors and edgy advertising.

Their recent foray into healthier baked chips demonstrates a keen awareness of evolving / rapidly changing consumer preferences.

However, their aggressive expansion strategy has led to increased debt, and they face stiff competition from smaller, more agile snack brands. Their market share currently stands at 32%, with a year-over-year growth rate of 8%.

Their stock price, while volatile, has shown impressive gains over the past five years, reflecting their higher risk profile and growth potential. However, their debt levels are a concern, and their future success hinges on their ability to maintain their innovative edge and fend off smaller competitors.

Zesty Crackers, the established giant, enjoys a legacy of quality and consistency. Their classic cracker varieties are a pantry staple in many Economia households, providing a rock-solid customer / fan base.

However, their product line is perceived as somewhat outdated, and their marketing efforts lag behind their competitors. They hold the largest market share at 41%, but their growth has plateaued at around 2% annually. Their stock price has shown steady, albeit modest, growth over the past decade, reflecting their stability and established market position. However, their lack of innovation and slow adaptation to changing consumer trends pose a threat to their long-term dominance.

Sweet Biscuits, the purveyor of premium treats, caters to a more discerning palate. Their indulgent cookies and pastries command a higher price point, attracting a loyal affluent clientele. Their brand is synonymous with luxury and quality.

However, their reliance on high-end products makes them vulnerable to economic downturns, and their market share, while a respectable 21%, has been declining slightly due to increased competition in the premium snack segment. Their stock price has seen periods of high growth interspersed with periods of stagnation, reflecting the cyclical nature of the luxury goods market.

Now, imagine you have $10,000 to invest. You've done your research, analyzed the financial statements of each company, and you're impressed by all three.

Crunchy Chips promises high growth, but carries more risk. Zesty Crackers offers stability, but limited growth. Sweet Biscuits provides premium appeal, but vulnerability to economic fluctuations.

- Crunchy Chips has a profit margin of 12%,
- Zesty Crackers 15% and
- Sweet Biscuits 10%.

Which company do you choose? This is the classic investor's dilemma.

Each company presents a compelling case. Crunchy Chips, with its youthful appeal and innovative products, seems poised for rapid expansion. Zesty Crackers, with its established brand and loyal customer base, offers a sense of security. Sweet Biscuits, with its premium offerings and strong brand recognition, promises high returns for those willing to weather the potential economic storms over time in the market.

Let's say, after careful consideration, you decide to invest in Zesty Crackers, drawn to their established brand and consistent performance. You're confident that they'll continue to deliver steady returns. You like their stability. You like their long history an the fact that it cover 41% of the market share.

But what about the other 59% of the market?

What about the smaller snack brands that are innovating and disrupting the industry? What if one of them becomes the next big snack sensation?

By choosing only Zesty Crackers, you're missing out on the potential growth of the rest of the market. You're limiting your investment potential.

You're also exposed to the risk that Zesty Crackers' growth stagnates even further, or that they lose market share to more aggressive competitors.

What if a new health craze sweeps Economia, and crackers fall out of favor? Your investment, concentrated in a single company, is exposed to significant risk.

This is where the true power of ETFs comes into play.

An Exchange Traded Fund (ETF) designed to track the Economia snack food market would allow you to invest in all three major players – Crunchy Chips, Zesty Crackers, and Sweet Biscuits – and also the smaller, emerging brands.

You're not just picking one company; you're investing in the entire snack food market in Economia.

You're participating in the overall growth of the industry, not just the fate of a single company.

You're diversifying your risk and maximizing your potential for long-term returns.

Think of it like this: instead of buying just one flavor of chips, you're buying the entire variety pack. You're diversifying your investment across the whole snack aisle, capturing the overall growth of the industry, regardless of which brand ultimately becomes the most popular. You're not trying to predict which snack will be the next big hit; you're investing in the success of the snack food market as a whole.

ETFs offer several key advantages:

Diversification: By investing in a basket of assets, you significantly reduce your risk. If one company underperforms, the others can balance out your returns.

In the case of our snack food market, if Zesty Crackers experiences a temporary setback, your investment in Crunchy Chips and Sweet Biscuits, as well as the smaller players, can help mitigate the impact.

You're not reliant on the performance of a single company. You're invested in the success of the entire market. This diversification is crucial for long-term investing success. It smooths out the ups and downs of individual stock performance and reduces the volatility of your portfolio.

Simplicity: ETF investing is incredibly simple. With a single trade, you can gain broad market exposure, saving you the time and effort of researching and picking individual stocks.

You can focus on your life, knowing that your investments are working for you, effortlessly. You don't need to spend hours analyzing financial statements or trying to predict which company will be the next big thing.

You're investing in the overall growth of the market, which is a much simpler and more efficient approach. This simplicity makes ETF investing accessible to everyone, regardless of their financial knowledge or experience. You don't need to be a Wall Street expert to understand and benefit from ETF investing.

Transparency: ETFs are typically very transparent. You can easily see the underlying holdings of the ETF, so you know exactly what you're invested in. This level of transparency can give you greater peace of mind. You can see the exact composition of the ETF's portfolio, including the percentage of assets allocated to each company or sector. This transparency allows you to make informed decisions about your investments and understand the risks and potential rewards associated with each holding.

You're not investing in a black box; you know exactly where your money is going.

Liquidity: ETFs trade on stock exchanges like individual stocks, which means they're highly liquid. You can buy and sell shares of an ETF quickly and easily, often at very low transaction costs.

This liquidity gives you flexibility and control over your investments. If you need to access your money, you can typically sell your ETF shares without difficulty. This is a significant advantage over some other types of investments, which can be illiquid and difficult to sell.

So, the next time you're tempted to pick the "winning" stock, remember the snack food market in Economia. Consider the power of investing in the whole market through ETFs, rather than trying to predict the future.

Instead of betting on a single company, you're betting on the growth and success of the overall market. You're diversifying your risk, minimizing your costs, and simplifying your investment strategy. Let's revisit our snack food market analogy one last time.

Imagine that over the next five years, the snack food market in Economia experiences significant growth. New and innovative snack brands emerge, capturing a larger share of the market. Consumer preferences shift, and some of the older, established brands lose market share.

If you had invested solely in Zesty Crackers, you would have missed out on the growth of the emerging brands and potentially seen your returns stagnate.

However, if you had invested in the Economia Snack Food ETF, you would have captured the growth of the entire market, including the up-and-coming snack companies. You would have benefited from the overall expansion of the snack food industry, regardless of which individual companies ultimately emerged as the "winner."

This is the beauty of ETF investing. It allows you to participate in the growth of the market / segment / region / category without having to predict the future or pick individual stocks. It's a smarter, more strategic approach to building wealth over the long term.

In the following chapters, we'll delve deeper into the world of ETFs, exploring different types and strategies to help you build a truly effortless and successful investment portfolio.

We'll look at country-specific ETFs, sector-specific ETFs, purpose-driven ETFs, and even global ETFs, showing you how to diversify your investments and achieve your financial goals without the stress and uncertainty of individual stock picking.

We'll also explore the important topic of asset allocation, which is the foundation of any successful investment strategy.

And, of course, we'll delve into the specifics of the "mystery ETF" I mentioned in the introduction, the one that can give you broad exposure to the global market with a single investment.

By the end of this book, you'll have a clear understanding of how ETFs can simplify your investing, reduce your risk, and help you achieve your financial dreams.

You'll be able to make informed decisions about your investments, confident in the knowledge that you're taking a long-term, strategic approach to building wealth. You'll be able to sleep soundly at night, knowing that your money is working for you, even while you're not actively managing your portfolio. You'll be free from the stress and anxiety of trying to time the market or pick the "winning" stock.

Let's begin this journey of transformation from someone who invests harder to someone who invests smarter – making you "*The Effortless Investor*".

CHAPTER 2

Beyond Your Borders: The Power of Country-Specific ETFs

"Why limit yourself to one country when the world offers so many opportunities?" That's a question I've often pondered throughout my life. My journey has taken me from India, my birth country, to the United Kingdom for my MBA, and finally to Canada, where I've chosen to build my life. Along the way, I've had the privilege of visiting over 16 countries, each with its own unique culture, economy, and business landscape.

During my time across the world, I witnessed firsthand the incredible diversity of businesses and innovations that exist around the world. I saw solutions to problems that were unique to those countries, and I also observed needs that were unmet in some places but well-addressed in others. This global perspective ignited a passion within me – a passion for understanding different markets and seeking opportunities beyond my own borders.

This passion isn't just about travel or cultural experiences; it's also about smart investing. As investors, we often fall into the trap of focusing solely on our home markets. We invest in what we know, what's familiar, and what's comfortable. But in doing so, we may be missing out on significant growth opportunities and exposing our portfolios to unnecessary risk.

The Importance of International Diversification:

In the world of finance, diversification is a fundamental principle. It's the idea that by spreading your investments across different assets, you can reduce your overall risk. Just as you wouldn't put all your eggs in one basket, you shouldn't put all your investment dollars into a single country.

Here's why:
Reduced Risk: Different countries have different economic cycles. When one economy is booming, another might be struggling. By investing in a variety of countries, you can smooth out your returns and reduce the impact of any single country's poor performance on your overall portfolio. This concept is supported by extensive research that demonstrates how lower correlations between international markets can significantly decrease portfolio volatility.

Access to Growth Opportunities: The global economy is vast and dynamic. Some countries offer faster growth rates than others. Emerging markets, for example, often have rapidly expanding economies and a growing middle class, which can translate to higher returns for investors. By investing internationally, you gain access to these growth opportunities that may not be available in your home market.

Currency Diversification: Investing in different countries also means investing in different currencies. Currency values fluctuate, and holding a mix of currencies can provide a hedge against inflation and economic uncertainty in your home country. For instance, a Canadian investor holding US and European assets benefits from currency diversification. If the Canadian dollar weakens, the value of their holdings in other currencies will increase, potentially offsetting losses in their domestic investments.

Introduction to Country-Specific ETFs

So, how can the average investor easily diversify their portfolio internationally? The answer lies in country-specific Exchange-Traded Funds (ETFs).

A country-specific ETF is a type of investment fund that focuses on tracking a specific country's stock market index. For example, a Canadian investor who wants to invest in Japan can buy an ETF that tracks the Japanese Topix index. This ETF will hold a basket of Japanese stocks, providing the investor with diversified exposure to the Japanese market without having to buy individual stocks.

Country-specific ETFs offer a simple and cost-effective way to gain access to international markets. Instead of having to research and purchase individual stocks in foreign countries, investors can buy a single ETF that represents a broad cross-section of that country's economy.

Here are some examples of popular country-specific ETFs:

Developed Markets:

- EWC: iShares MSCI Canada ETF, providing exposure to the Canadian stock market.
- EWA: iShares MSCI Australia ETF, offering access to the Australian market.
- EWG: iShares MSCI Germany ETF, tracking the German equity market.
- EWJ: iShares MSCI Japan ETF, investing in Japanese stocks.
- EWU: iShares MSCI United Kingdom ETF, giving exposure to the UK market.

Emerging Markets:

- EEM: iShares MSCI Emerging Markets ETF, offering broad exposure to a basket of emerging economies.
- INDA: iShares MSCI India ETF, focusing on the Indian stock market.
- MCHI: iShares MSCI China ETF, providing access to Chinese equities.
- EWZ: iShares MSCI Brazil ETF

For beginner investors, country-specific ETFs are a game-changer. I remember when some of my friends in India were keen to invest in the US market but were unsure how to navigate the complexities of foreign stock exchanges, different regulations, and currency exchange. ETFs like those tracking the S&P 500 or Nasdaq 100 simplified the process, allowing them to participate in the US market with ease. Similarly, someone in Canada can easily invest in the Indian stock market through ETFs like INDA, without having to worry about the intricacies of the Indian financial system.

Risks and Rewards of Country-Specific ETFs:

Like any investment, country-specific ETFs come with their own set of potential risks and rewards. It's crucial to understand these factors before making any investment decisions.

Potential Rewards:

- Higher Growth Potential: Some countries, particularly emerging markets, have the potential for rapid economic growth. As these economies expand, their stock markets can deliver substantial returns for investors.
- Diversification Benefits: As mentioned earlier, country-specific ETFs can enhance portfolio diversification, reducing overall risk and improving risk-adjusted returns.
- Specific Market Exposure: These ETFs allow investors to target specific countries or regions that they believe have strong growth prospects.

Key Risks:

- Political Risk: Political instability, changes in government policies, and regulatory shifts can significantly impact a country's stock market. For example, a sudden change in leadership or unfavorable policy changes can lead to market volatility and decreased investor confidence.

- Economic Risk: Economic downturns, recessions, inflation, and interest rate fluctuations can affect a country's economy and its stock market. For instance, a country experiencing a recession may see its stock market decline, impacting the value of its country-specific ETF.

- Currency Risk: Currency exchange rates can be volatile, and changes in these rates can affect the returns of international investments. For Canadian investors, for example, if the Canadian dollar rises against the Japanese yen, the returns on a Japanese ETF (like EWJ) will be lower when translated back into Canadian dollars.

- Emerging Market Risks: Investing in emerging market ETFs carries additional risks, such as lower liquidity (ease of buying and selling), less transparency in financial reporting, and weaker corporate governance standards.

Mitigating the Risks:

While these risks are real, they can be managed. Here are some strategies for mitigating the risks associated with country-specific ETFs:

- Diversify Across Countries: Don't put all your international investment in a single country. Spread your investments across a range of countries and regions to reduce the impact of any one country's poor performance.
- Understand Country-Specific Risks: Before investing in a country-specific ETF, take the time to research the country's political and economic situation. Understand the potential risks and how they might affect your investment.
- Consider Your Risk Tolerance: Country-specific ETFs can be more volatile than broad market ETFs. Make sure your investment aligns with your risk tolerance and investment time horizon.

Country-Specific ETFs in an Effortless Portfolio:
Country-specific ETFs can play a valuable role in an "effortless" investing strategy. They offer a convenient and diversified way to gain exposure to international markets without the complexities of buying individual foreign stocks.

Imagine you're building a long-term investment portfolio. You could start with a foundation of broad market ETFs, such as:

- A Canadian ETF that tracks the S&P/TSX Composite Index.
- A US ETF that tracks the S&P 500.
- An international developed markets ETF.
- An emerging markets ETF.

This combination provides you with diversified exposure to the Canadian, US, and global stock markets. To further fine-tune your portfolio and potentially enhance returns, you could then add country-specific ETFs.

For example, if you believe that a particular country has strong growth prospects, you could allocate a portion of your portfolio to a country-specific ETF that tracks that market. This allows you to overweight that country in your portfolio and potentially benefit from its outperformance.

A Personal Example:
During my time in the UK for my MBA, I had the opportunity to witness the rapid growth of several emerging economies. I remember being particularly impressed by the dynamism of the Indian market. Having grown up in India, I understood the country's potential, but seeing it from a global perspective gave me a new appreciation for its growth trajectory.

I decided to invest a portion of my savings in an India-focused ETF. Over the next few years, India's economy expanded significantly, driven by factors such as a growing middle class, increasing urbanization, and a thriving technology sector. As a result, my investment in the India ETF generated substantial returns, significantly boosting my overall portfolio performance.

This experience not only reinforced the importance of international diversification but also highlighted the potential of country-specific ETFs to capture specific growth opportunities. While this investment proved successful, it's important to remember that all investments carry risk, and past performance is not indicative of future results.

Factors to Consider When Choosing a Country-Specific ETF:
When selecting a country-specific ETF, consider the following factors:

- Expense Ratio: This is the annual fee you'll pay to own the ETF. Lower expense ratios are better, as they eat less into your returns.
- Liquidity: This refers to how easily you can buy and sell the ETF. Higher liquidity means you can trade the ETF quickly and at a favorable price.
- Tracking Error: This measures how closely the ETF's performance matches the performance of its underlying index. A lower tracking error indicates that the ETF is doing a good job of tracking its index.
- Underlying Index: Understand the index that the ETF tracks. What companies are included in the index, and how is the index weighted?
- Fund Provider: Consider the reputation and experience of the company that manages the ETF.

Considerations for Canadian Readers / Investors:

For Canadian investors, there are some additional factors to keep in mind when investing in country-specific ETFs:

- Currency Exchange: When you invest in a foreign ETF, you're also investing in a foreign currency. Changes in exchange rates can impact your returns when you convert them back to Canadian dollars. You can manage this risk by: Holding a diversified portfolio of international ETFs with different currency exposures. Considering currency-hedged ETFs, which aim to minimize the impact of currency fluctuations.

- Tax Implications: Investing in foreign ETFs can have tax implications for Canadian investors. It's essential to understand how foreign dividends and capital gains are taxed in Canada. Generally, capital gains are taxed when you sell the ETF, while dividends may be taxed in the year they are received. It's always best to consult with a qualified tax advisor for personalized advice.

- Canadian-Listed ETFs: Canadian investors can often find Canadian-listed ETFs that provide exposure to international markets. These ETFs may offer some advantages, such as trading in Canadian dollars and potentially lower transaction costs.

Chapter Summary:

In today's interconnected world, limiting your investments to your home country can mean missing out on significant opportunities and exposing yourself to unnecessary risk. Country-specific ETFs offer a simple, efficient, and cost-effective way to diversify your portfolio internationally and gain exposure to the growth potential of various countries around the globe.

By understanding the benefits and risks of country-specific ETFs, and by carefully considering factors such as expense ratios, liquidity, and currency risk, you can make informed investment decisions that align with your financial goals.

Key Takeaway:

Don't let borders limit your investment potential. Explore the world of country-specific ETFs and discover the opportunities that lie beyond your home country.

With careful research and a diversified approach, you can build a more resilient and potentially more rewarding investment portfolio. Remember, you don't need to be an expert to invest globally; ETFs make it "effortless."

CHAPTER 3

Sector Surfing & Thematic Investing:

Riding the Waves of Industry and Trends

In the dynamic world of investing, it's crucial to identify not just individual companies, but also the broader trends and industries that are shaping the future. This chapter delves into two powerful strategies that can help you do just that: sector investing and thematic investing.

As an investor, you're constantly seeking ways to navigate the ever-changing market landscape and position your portfolio for long-term growth. While stock picking can be exciting, it's often complex and time-consuming. Sector and thematic investing offer a more streamlined approach, allowing you to capitalize on the potential of entire industries and transformative trends.

Defining Sector and Thematic Investing:
To understand these strategies, let's first define what we mean by "sector" and "theme."

Sector Investing Explained:

Sector investing involves focusing your investments on companies within a specific segment of the economy. These segments, or sectors, represent distinct areas of business activity.

Here are some common examples of sectors:

- *Technology: Companies involved in software, hardware, internet services, and other tech-related activities.*
- *Healthcare: Companies that provide medical services, pharmaceuticals, medical devices, and biotechnology.*
- *Energy: Companies that produce, refine, and distribute oil, gas, and other energy sources.*
- *Financials: Banks, insurance companies, investment firms, and other businesses that provide financial services.*
- *Consumer Staples: Companies that produce essential goods like food, beverages, and household products.*

Each sector tends to perform differently based on economic cycles. For example, consumer staples tend to be more resilient during economic downturns, as people still need to buy food and household necessities. Technology companies, on the other hand, may thrive during periods of economic expansion and technological innovation.

Thematic Investing Explained:

Thematic investing takes a broader perspective, focusing on long-term, structural trends that are transforming the global economy. These themes often cut across traditional sector classifications and represent powerful forces that are reshaping how we live, work, and interact.

Here are some compelling examples of thematic investment themes:

- Artificial Intelligence (AI): The development of intelligent machines and software that can perform tasks that typically require human intelligence. This theme spans across technology, healthcare, manufacturing, and many other sectors.

- Clean Energy: The transition from fossil fuels to renewable energy sources like solar, wind, and hydro power. This theme involves companies in the energy, utilities, and technology sectors.

- E-commerce: The growth of online shopping and the shift away from traditional brick-and-mortar retail. This theme primarily involves the technology and consumer discretionary sectors.

- Aging Population: The increasing proportion of elderly people in many developed countries, creating demand for healthcare, pharmaceuticals, and other related products and services. This theme mainly involves the healthcare sector.

- Cybersecurity: The growing need to protect computer systems and networks from cyberattacks, driving demand for cybersecurity software and services.

Thematic investing is about identifying and investing in these transformative trends early on, positioning your portfolio to benefit from their long-term growth.

Distinguishing the Two:

While both sector and thematic investing involve focusing on specific areas of the market, there's a key distinction:

Sector investing focuses on industries, which are classifications based on the type of business activity.

Thematic investing focuses on broader trends, which can span multiple industries and represent fundamental shifts in the global economy.

In essence, sector investing is about "where" companies operate, while thematic investing is about "why" certain areas of the economy are growing.

The Importance of Sector and Thematic Investing:

Both sector and thematic investing offer unique benefits for investors:

- Targeted Exposure: Sector investing allows you to fine-tune your portfolio and gain targeted exposure to specific areas of the economy that you believe will outperform. For example, if you anticipate a rise in interest rates, you might increase your allocation to the financials sector.

- Cyclical Opportunities: As mentioned earlier, different sectors perform differently during various phases of the economic cycle. Sector investing allows you to potentially capitalize on these cyclical trends.

Benefits of Thematic Investing:

- Growth Potential: Thematic investing provides the opportunity to invest in powerful, long-term trends that have the potential to generate significant growth. For instance, the rise of AI is expected to transform numerous industries, and investors who position themselves early on could reap substantial rewards.

- Future-Oriented: Thematic investing is about looking ahead and positioning your portfolio for the future. It's about investing in the companies and industries that are driving innovation and shaping the world of tomorrow.

My Perspective:

I've always found sector-specific ETFs particularly intriguing. When I first came across an ETF like CHPS, which tracks major semiconductor chip companies like Nvidia, I was amazed at how easily investors could gain exposure to such a critical industry. As someone keenly following the advancements in Artificial Intelligence, I recognized the pivotal role of semiconductor chips in powering this technology. Sector-specific ETFs like CHPS provide a straightforward way to "play" the AI tarend without having to pick individual winners.

Similarly, there are ETFs that track the electric vehicle (EV) industry, clean energy, and other exciting sectors. These ETFs offer investors the opportunity to participate in the growth of these industries without having to become experts in each individual company.

Exploring Key Sectors and Themes:

Let's delve deeper into some key sectors and themes that are shaping the investment landscape:

Key Sectors:

- Technology: This sector continues to be a driving force of innovation, with artificial intelligence, and cybersecurity being key growth areas. Companies like Microsoft, Amazon (AWS), and Google (Google Cloud) dominate the cloud computing space, while companies like Nvidia and Intel are at the forefront of AI chip development. The increasing reliance on technology also drives demand for cybersecurity solutions, benefiting companies like Palo Alto Networks and CrowdStrike.

- Healthcare: An aging global population and advancements in medical technology are driving growth in the healthcare sector. Areas like biotechnology, pharmaceuticals, and medical devices offer long-term investment potential. Companies like Johnson & Johnson, Pfizer, and Abbott Laboratories are major players in this sector.
- Energy: While traditional energy sources still play a significant role, the transition to renewable energy is accelerating. Companies involved in solar, wind, and other clean energy technologies are poised for growth. Companies like NextEra Energy and Vestas Wind Systems are key players in this space.
- Financials: The financial sector is influenced by factors such as interest rates, economic growth, and regulatory changes. Companies like JPMorgan Chase, Bank of America, and Visa are major players in this sector.
- Consumer Staples: This sector provides essential goods and services that consumers need regardless of the economic climate. Companies like Procter & Gamble, Coca-Cola, and Walmart are considered consumer staples.
- Electric Vehicles (EVs): This sub-sector within the broader automotive industry is experiencing rapid growth, driven by

increasing environmental awareness and technological advancements. Companies like Tesla are leading the charge, but traditional automakers like Volkswagen and General Motors are also investing heavily in EVs.

- Semiconductors: As mentioned earlier, the semiconductor industry is crucial for powering many technological advancements, including AI, 5G, and cloud computing. Companies like Nvidia, Intel, and Taiwan Semiconductor Manufacturing Company (TSMC) are key players in this sector.

Compelling Themes:

- Artificial Intelligence (AI): AI is transforming industries across the board, from healthcare and finance to transportation and entertainment. Companies that are developing and implementing AI technologies are expected to see significant growth in the coming years.

- Clean Energy: The global shift towards renewable energy sources is creating a massive investment opportunity. Companies involved in solar, wind, hydro, and other clean energy technologies are poised for long-term growth.

- E-commerce: The growth of online shopping continues to disrupt traditional retail, with companies like Amazon leading the way. The e-commerce theme also encompasses related areas like logistics, online payments, and digital marketing.

- Aging Population: As the global population ages, the demand for healthcare, pharmaceuticals, and senior care services is increasing. Companies in these industries are expected to benefit from this demographic trend.

- Cybersecurity: With the increasing reliance on technology and the growing threat of cyberattacks, the demand for cybersecurity solutions is soaring. Companies that provide cybersecurity software and services are expected to see strong growth.

My Personal Experience:

Navigating the AI Boom: The recent surge in interest surrounding Artificial Intelligence provides a compelling example of the challenges and opportunities of thematic investing.

When AI burst into the mainstream consciousness with the rise of large language models and generative AI, the market went into a frenzy. Nvidia, a leading manufacturer of the GPUs that power these AI systems, saw its stock price skyrocket.

Like many investors, I recognized the transformative potential of AI. However, I also remembered the wisdom of legendary investor Warren Buffett: "Be fearful when others are greedy, and greedy when others are fearful." While everyone was rushing to buy Nvidia, I hesitated. I felt that the stock price had become detached from its intrinsic value, driven more by hype than fundamentals.

In the months that followed, Nvidia's stock price experienced significant volatility. While it continued to climb for a while, it eventually experienced a sharp correction. Even after the pullback, I still felt that the stock was richly valued.

At the same time, I recognized that Nvidia wasn't the only player in the AI space. Advanced Micro Devices (AMD) also produces GPUs and CPUs that are used in AI applications. While AMD wasn't as dominant as Nvidia, it was still a significant player in the industry.

However, I faced a dilemma. I didn't want to invest all my money in Nvidia at what I perceived to be an inflated price. But I also didn't want to miss out on the AI opportunity altogether by investing solely in AMD, which, while promising, didn't have the same market position as Nvidia.

My solution was to invest in a semiconductor ETF that held both Nvidia and AMD, along with other companies in the semiconductor industry.

This strategy offered several advantages:

- Diversified Exposure: By investing in an ETF, I gained exposure to a basket of semiconductor companies, reducing my reliance on the performance of any single stock.

- Balanced Portfolio: The ETF's holdings were weighted in such a way that the strengths of one company helped to offset the weaknesses of another. For example, Nvidia's dominance in the high-end GPU market was balanced by AMD's presence in other segments.

- Risk Management: This approach helped to mitigate risk. While my portfolio benefited from the overall growth of the AI sector, it was less vulnerable to the volatility of any single stock.

While my returns may not have been as spectacular as those of investors who went all-in on Nvidia at the very beginning, my portfolio was also much more resilient during periods of market turbulence. This experience reinforced my belief in the power of diversification and the importance of taking a balanced approach to investing, even in high-growth sectors.

Risks and Challenges of Sector and Thematic Investing:

While sector and thematic investing can be rewarding, it's essential to be aware of the potential risks and challenges:

- Sector-Specific Volatility: Sector ETFs can be more volatile than broad market ETFs, as their performance is tied to the fortunes of a specific industry. For example, an energy ETF can be highly sensitive to fluctuations in oil prices.

- Overvaluation: Thematic investing, in particular, can be susceptible to overvaluation. When a theme becomes popular, investor enthusiasm can drive up the prices of companies related to that theme, creating a bubble.

- Theme Concentration: Concentrating your portfolio in a single theme can be risky. If that theme doesn't play out as expected, or if it falls out of favor with investors, you could suffer significant losses.

- Obsolescence Risk: Some themes may not be as long-lasting as they seem. Technological advancements or unforeseen events can disrupt even the most promising trends.

- Lack of Diversification: Overweighting specific sectors or themes can reduce the overall diversification of your portfolio, making it more vulnerable to market downturns.

Mitigating the Risks:

Fortunately, there are several ways to mitigate these risks:

- Diversification: The most important risk management tool is diversification. Don't put all your eggs in one basket.

Spread your investments across different sectors, themes, and asset classes.

- Due Diligence: Thoroughly research the sectors and themes you're interested in. Understand the underlying trends, the key players, and the potential risks and rewards.

- Long-Term Perspective: Thematic investing, in particular, requires a long-term perspective. These themes often take years, or even decades, to fully play out. Be prepared to ride out short-term volatility.

- Regular Review: Periodically review your sector and thematic investments to ensure they still align with your investment goals and risk tolerance. Be willing to adjust your portfolio as market conditions and your outlook change.

Sector and Thematic ETFs in an "Effortless" Investing Strategy:
Sector and thematic ETFs can be powerful tools for implementing an "effortless" investing strategy. They allow you to gain diversified exposure to specific industries or trends without having to constantly research and trade individual stocks.

Instead of trying to pick the "best" companies within a sector or theme, you can simply invest in an ETF that tracks that sector or theme.

This approach offers several advantages:

- Simplicity: ETFs are easy to buy and sell, just like individual stocks.
- Diversification: A single ETF can provide exposure to dozens or even hundreds of companies within a sector or theme.
- Cost-Effectiveness: ETFs typically have low expense ratios, making them a cost-efficient way to gain diversified exposure.

You can combine sector and thematic ETFs with broad market ETFs to build a diversified portfolio that captures specific trends and opportunities. For example, you could combine a US total market ETF with a clean energy ETF and a cybersecurity ETF to create a portfolio that is diversified across the broad market but also tilted towards these high-growth themes.

Factors to Consider When Choosing Sector and Thematic ETFs:

When selecting sector or thematic ETFs, consider the following factors:

- Expense Ratios: As with any ETF, pay close attention to the expense ratio. Lower expense ratios mean more of your investment returns go into your pocket.

- Tracking Error: This measures how closely the ETF's performance matches the performance of its underlying index. A lower tracking error indicates that the ETF is doing a good job of tracking its target sector or theme.

- Fund Composition: Look at the specific companies held within the ETF and their weightings. Ensure that the ETF aligns with your investment goals and risk tolerance.

- Concentration Risk: Some sector or thematic ETFs may be heavily concentrated in a few holdings. This can increase volatility and reduce diversification.

- Liquidity: Choose ETFs that are actively traded, as this will make it easier to buy and sell shares at a fair price.

- Index Methodology: Understand the rules and criteria used to construct the underlying index that the ETF tracks.

Examples of Successful Sector / Thematic Investing:

- Technology in the late 90s and 2000s: The late 1990s and early 2000s saw the explosive growth of the internet and the dot-com boom. Investors who recognized this trend early on and invested in technology stocks or technology-focused ETFs experienced substantial returns. While the dot-com bubble eventually burst, the long-term growth of the internet and technology has been undeniable.

- The rise of e-commerce: The growth of e-commerce, led by companies like Amazon, has transformed the retail landscape. Investors who identified this trend and invested in e-commerce companies or ETFs have benefited from the shift away from traditional brick-and-mortar retail. From 1997 to 2023, Amazon's stock grew from approximately $1.50 to $130, showcasing the massive returns possible from investing in a transformative theme.

- The growth of clean energy: As the world increasingly focuses on combating climate change, the demand for clean energy solutions is surging. Investors who recognized this trend and invested in companies or ETFs focused on solar, wind, and other renewable energy sources have the potential for significant long-term gains. For example, the Invesco WilderHill Clean Energy ETF (PBW) has shown substantial growth since its inception, reflecting the increasing investor interest in this sector.

Chapter Summary:

Sector and thematic investing provide investors with powerful tools to navigate the complexities of the modern market. By focusing on specific industries and long-term trends, investors can potentially enhance their portfolio's diversification and capture significant growth opportunities.

While these strategies come with their own set of risks, a diversified approach, thorough research, and a long-term perspective can help investors mitigate these risks and achieve their financial goals.

Key Takeaway:

Instead of focusing solely on individual stocks, consider the broader sectors and themes that are shaping the global economy. Sector and thematic ETFs offer a convenient and cost-effective way to gain diversified exposure to these trends, allowing you to "ride the waves" of economic growth and innovation.

For example, instead of trying to pick the single best company in an industry, you can invest in an ETF that holds all the major players, capturing the growth of the entire sector.

CHAPTER 4

Going Global: Building Your Worldwide ETF Portfolio

In today's interconnected world, limiting your investments to your home country can mean missing out on significant growth opportunities. Global diversification, the practice of investing across different countries, has become essential for building a resilient and high-performing portfolio. This chapter will guide you through the process of constructing a diversified global ETF portfolio, with a special focus on a powerful, all-in-one ETF strategy.

The Case for Global Diversification:
"Don't put all your eggs in one basket" is an age-old adage that holds particularly true in investing. Diversification, spreading your investments across various assets, sectors, and countries, is crucial for reducing risk and enhancing returns.

The Importance of Diversification:
Diversification works by reducing your portfolio's exposure to any single asset or market. When one investment performs poorly, others may perform well, offsetting the losses. This smoothing effect can help to minimize volatility and improve your overall investment experience.

Home Country Bias:

Despite the clear benefits of diversification, many investors exhibit a phenomenon known as "home country bias." This is the tendency to over-allocate their investments to their home country's stock market, even when other markets offer attractive opportunities.

Home country bias can stem from several factors, including:

- Familiarity: Investors tend to be more comfortable investing in companies and markets they know well.
- Optimism: Investors may be overly optimistic about their home country's economic prospects.
- Accessibility: Investing in foreign markets can sometimes seem complex or expensive.

However, relying too heavily on your home market can expose your portfolio to significant risks. If your country's economy experiences a downturn, your investments could suffer.

Growth Potential in Emerging Markets:

One of the strongest arguments for global diversification is the potential for higher growth in emerging markets. Emerging market economies, such as China, India, and Brazil, often grow at a faster pace than developed economies. This growth can translate into higher returns for investors.

To illustrate this point, let's consider the historical performance of developed and emerging markets. Over the past 10 years, from 2014 to 2023, the MSCI Emerging Markets Index has shown substantial growth, driven by factors such as rising incomes, increasing urbanization, and technological advancements. While developed markets, as represented by the MSCI World Index, have also delivered solid returns, emerging markets have, at times, demonstrated the potential for higher growth.

As the saying goes, "*The tree that is already tall has less room to grow than the sapling*." This captures the essence of investing in markets with high growth potential. While developed markets offer stability and established companies, emerging markets provide the opportunity to participate in economies that are still in the early stages of development.

Benefits of Global Investing:

In summary, global investing offers several key benefits:

- Wider range of investment opportunities: Access to companies and industries not available in your home market.
- Reduced risk through diversification: Lower volatility and more stable returns.
- Potential for higher returns: Participation in the growth of faster-growing economies.

Understanding Global ETFs:

Global ETFs provide a simple and cost-effective way to achieve international diversification.

What are Global ETFs?

A global ETF is an exchange-traded fund that invests in a portfolio of stocks from various countries around the world. Unlike single-country ETFs, which focus on a specific nation, or regional ETFs, which concentrate on a particular geographic area (such as Europe or Asia), global ETFs aim to provide broad exposure to the entire global stock market.

Benefits and Risks of Global ETFs:

Global ETFs offer several advantages:

- Broad diversification: Instant access to a diversified portfolio of international stocks.
- Simplified international investing: No need to research and trade individual stocks in foreign markets.
- Cost-effectiveness: Typically have lower expense ratios than actively managed international mutual funds.

However, it's essential to be aware of the risks involved:

- Currency risk: Fluctuations in exchange rates can impact the value of your investment.
- Political and economic risks: Political instability, economic downturns, or regulatory changes in foreign countries can affect stock prices.

- Tracking error: The ETF's performance may not perfectly match the performance of its underlying index.

Global ETFs for Different Investment Goals:
Global ETFs can be valuable tools for achieving a variety of investment objectives. As I discussed in my debut book, "The Game of Percentage: A Simple Guide to Actually Grow Your Money," a core principle of successful investing is aligning your investment strategy with your personal financial goals.

Global ETFs can be used to pursue goals like:

- Long-term growth: By providing exposure to a wide range of global companies, these ETFs allow investors to participate in the long-term growth of the global economy.
- Income generation: Some global ETFs focus on dividend-paying stocks, providing investors with a steady stream of income. Investors can look into Global Dividend ETFs for such focused investments.
- Risk management: The diversification offered by global ETFs can help to reduce portfolio volatility and manage risk.

Selecting Global ETFs: When choosing a global ETF, it's crucial to consider several factors:

- Expense ratios: Lower expense ratios can significantly boost your long-term returns.
- Liquidity: Higher trading volume makes it easier to buy and sell ETF shares.

- Diversification: Ensure the ETF provides broad diversification across countries and sectors. Examine the ETF's holdings to avoid excessive overlap with your existing investments.

- Underlying Index: Understand the methodology of the index the ETF tracks. This will help you determine the ETF's investment strategy and risk profile.

- Currency Risk: Investing in global ETFs exposes you to currency risk. When the value of foreign currencies declines relative to your home currency, your returns can be reduced.

Managing Currency Risk

Here are some strategies for managing currency risk:

- Diversification: Holding a diversified portfolio of global ETFs with different currency exposures can help to mitigate the impact of any single currency's fluctuations.

- Currency-hedged ETFs: These ETFs use financial instruments to minimize the impact of currency movements on their returns. While they can reduce currency risk, they may also have higher expense ratios.

The "Mystery" ETF:

A Comprehensive Global Solution One of the most effective ways to build a global ETF portfolio is to use a single ETF that provides broad exposure to major equity markets worldwide. This type of ETF offers a convenient, all-in-one solution for investors seeking diversified global equity exposure.

Characteristics: These ETFs typically invest in a diversified portfolio of stocks from both developed and emerging markets, and could include everything in between. They cover a wide range of countries and sectors, providing investors with a truly global perspective. The specific holdings and their weightings will vary depending on the ETF, but the goal is to mirror the performance of the global stock market.

Many of these ETFs use a market-capitalization-weighted approach, where the largest companies in each market receive the highest weightings in the portfolio. However, some ETFs may use alternative weighting methodologies, such as equal weighting, which gives each company in the index the same weight.

My Experience with the "mystery" ETF:

In my own investing journey, I've found that using a single, diversified global equity ETF has greatly simplified the process of international investing.

For instance, an ETF like *XEQT* provides Canadian investors with diversified exposure. It has allowed me to gain exposure to markets around the world without having to worry about selecting individual countries or regions.

Benefits:

The benefits of using this type of global ETF are numerous:

- Simplicity: A single purchase provides instant diversification across the global equity market.
- Convenience: It eliminates the need to manage multiple ETFs or individual stocks.
- Broad diversification: Reduces the risk associated with investing in any single country or region.
- Cost-effectiveness: These ETFs typically have low expense ratios.
- Effortless investing: This approach aligns perfectly with the concept of "effortless" investing by providing a hands-off way to achieve global equity exposure.

For Non-North American Readers:

If you're not based in the US & Canada, I encourage you to research similar all-in-one global equity ETFs available in your country.

Look for ETFs that offer broad market coverage, low expense ratios, and a diversified portfolio of holdings. These ETFs can provide you with a simple and effective way to build a diversified global equity portfolio.

Building an Effortless Global Portfolio:

Global ETFs can form the foundation of an effortless investment strategy.

By combining them with other ETFs that track different asset classes, such as bonds or real estate, you can create a diversified portfolio that aligns with your risk tolerance and financial goals.

Simple Allocation Models:

Here are two simple yet effective portfolio allocation models that utilize global ETFs:

- *60/40 Portfolio:* A classic allocation that aims to balance growth and stability.

60% Global Equity ETF: Provides diversified exposure to the global stock market.
40% Bond ETF: Offers stability and income through investments in bonds.

- *Three-Fund Portfolio:* A simple and efficient portfolio that covers the major asset classes.

1. Global Equity ETF: For global stock market exposure.
2. Bond ETF: For bond market exposure.
3. REIT ETF: For exposure to real estate.

The specific allocation percentages can be adjusted based on your individual circumstances and risk tolerance.

Staying the Course: Regardless of the specific allocation you choose, it's crucial to maintain a long-term perspective. Global markets can be volatile in the short term, but over the long run, a well-diversified global portfolio has historically provided solid returns.

Why This Changes Everything: My "Aha!" Moment:
I want to take a moment to talk about why this concept of a single, globally diversified equity ETF is, in my opinion, a game-changer for long-term investors.

Early in my investing journey, I, like many others, started with a more complicated approach. I had a collection of different ETFs, each tracking a specific country or region. I had my US ETFs, my Canadian ETFs, some emerging market exposure, and a separate Europe ETF. It was a lot to manage! I constantly worried about whether my allocations were correct, if I was missing out on some hot market, and the rebalancing process was a headache.

Then, I discovered ETFs like XEQT.

It was an "aha!" moment. I realized I could achieve the same (or even better) diversification with a single fund. All the developed and emerging markets, all the major sectors, all in one place. The simplicity was liberating. But it's not just about convenience. It's about the power of truly global diversification. When you look at the holdings of these ETFs, it's eye-opening. You're not just investing in the US or Canada; you're investing in the world's leading companies, across every sector, in every major economy. You're participating in global growth, no matter where it happens.

For Canadian investors, I'd suggest taking a close look at ETFs like XEQT. See its holdings. Examine its country and sector weightings. You'll see that it's a snapshot of the global economy. And for those of you outside Canada, I urge you to find similar ETFs in your own markets. They are out there, and they can truly simplify and enhance your investment strategy.

This, to me, is what "*effortless investing*" is all about. It's not about being lazy; it's about being smart. It's about using the tools available to us to achieve maximum diversification and long-term growth with minimal effort and stress.

This type of ETF, in my opinion, represents a huge leap forward for individual investors. It puts the power of global diversification within easy reach, allowing anyone to build a truly resilient and globally diversified portfolio.

Chapter Summary:

Global diversification is essential for building a resilient and high-performing portfolio. Global ETFs offer a simple and cost-effective way to achieve this diversification.

By understanding the benefits and risks of global investing, carefully selecting global ETFs, and avoiding common mistakes, you can construct a diversified global ETF portfolio that aligns with your long-term financial goals.

Key Takeaway:

Global diversification is crucial for reducing risk and enhancing returns. Global ETFs provide a simple and cost-effective way to invest in international markets.

Consider factors such as expense ratios, tracking error, and currency risk when selecting global ETFs.

A single, diversified global equity ETF can provide broad market exposure with ease.

Combine global ETFs with other asset class ETFs to create a well-rounded portfolio.

CHAPTER 5

Easy Portfolio: How to Allocate Your ETFs Like a Pro

(Including a section on Dividend ETFs)

Let's talk about building an "effortless" portfolio. You might think that means throwing your money into a few random investments and hoping for the best. But that's not it at all.

"*Effortless*" actually means setting up a smart system from the start, so you don't have to constantly stress about your investments later. And at the heart of that system is asset allocation.

Why Asset Allocation Matters (More Than Anything Else):
You know, people often get caught up in trying to find the next hot stock or time the market perfectly. They're constantly chasing quick wins, glued to their screens, and stressing over every little fluctuation.

But here's the thing: study after study has shown that asset allocation—how you divide your money across different asset classes—is far more important in determining your long-term returns.

Think of it like this: imagine you're building a house. You wouldn't just focus on the paint color and ignore the foundation, right? Asset allocation is the foundation of your investment portfolio. It's about building a structure that can weather different economic conditions and help you achieve your financial goals.

The Basic Building Blocks: Key Asset Classes:
So, what are these "asset classes" we keep talking about? They're basically categories of investments that tend to behave differently in the market.

Here are the main ones you should know:

- Stocks: These represent ownership in companies. They offer the potential for high growth but can also be volatile. Think of them as the engine of your portfolio, driving long-term returns.
- Bonds: These are essentially loans you make to governments or corporations. They tend to be less volatile than stocks and provide more stability and income. Consider them the ballast of your portfolio, providing stability and steady returns.
- Real Estate: This can include physical properties or investments in real estate companies. It can provide both income and capital appreciation, and can also act as a hedge against inflation.

- Cash: This includes things like savings accounts and money market funds. It's the safest asset class, but it typically offers the lowest returns. Think of it as your emergency fund, there for safety and quick access.

Your Personal Blueprint: Aligning Allocation with Your Goals

The right asset allocation for you depends on a few key factors:

- Age: If you're younger, you generally have a longer time horizon, so you can afford to take on more risk with a higher allocation to stocks. As you get closer to retirement, you might want to shift more towards bonds and other stable assets.
- Risk Tolerance: How comfortable are you with market swings? If you're the type to panic when your investments go down, you'll want a more conservative allocation with a higher percentage of bonds.
- Financial Goals: What are you saving for? Retirement, a down payment on a house, your children's education? Your goals will influence your time horizon and risk tolerance, which in turn will determine your ideal asset allocation.

Earning While You Own: The Magic of Dividend ETFs

Now, let's talk about a type of ETF that's near and dear to my heart: *Dividend ETFs*.

These are funds that invest in companies that pay out regular dividends to their shareholders.
And why am I so interested in dividends? Let me introduce you to a concept - and a quote - you might have heard of: compound interest.

You know that famous quote, often attributed to Albert Einstein, about compound interest being the "*eighth wonder of the world*"? Well, it's true, in my opinion.

Compound interest is a powerful force. When you reinvest your dividends, you're essentially earning returns on your returns. Over time, this can significantly boost your overall investment growth.

Dividend ETFs allow you to tap into this power. You get the potential for stock market growth, plus a stream of income in the form of dividends. Personally, I'm a big fan of reinvesting those dividends. It's like giving your investments an extra push, and it's something I highly respect.

There are different types of Dividend ETFs. Some focus on companies with a long history of increasing their dividends, while others target companies with high dividend yields.

The beauty of dividend ETFs is that they can provide both stable growth and a consistent income stream, which you can then reinvest to accelerate your wealth-building.

Beyond the Basics: Taking Your Allocation to the Next Level:
Once you're comfortable with the basic asset classes, you can explore more sophisticated allocation strategies using ETFs.

For example, you could: Tilt towards specific factors: As we discussed in the previous chapter, you can use ETFs to focus on factors like value, growth, or momentum, which have historically been associated with higher returns.

Diversify across sectors or themes: You can use ETFs to gain targeted exposure to specific sectors (like technology or healthcare) or themes (like clean energy or artificial intelligence).

The Importance of Rebalancing (and How to Do It Effortlessly):
Over time, your initial asset allocation will likely drift away from your target due to market movements. For example, if stocks perform really well, your portfolio might end up with a higher percentage of stocks than you originally intended.

That's where rebalancing comes in. It involves periodically bringing your portfolio back to its original allocation.

How often should you do it? There's no magic number. Some investors rebalance annually, others quarterly, and some only when their allocation deviates significantly from their target (say, by 5% or more).

The key is to be consistent and avoid trying to time the market. Rebalancing isn't about predicting the future; it's about maintaining your desired level of risk and return.

Investing with Confidence: Do Your Homework

Before you invest in any ETF, take the time to do your research. I can't stress this enough. You need to be confident in your investment decisions, so you can stick with them through thick and thin.

Here's my personal philosophy: I believe in doing thorough research before I invest. I want to understand what I'm buying, how it works, and what the potential risks and rewards are. Because once I've made an investment, I want to be able to stay calm and focused, even when the market gets choppy.

In fact, I actually get happy when the stock market goes down. Let me give you an example. Imagine you want to buy something - an apple for instance. If it costs $5 today, and tomorrow it costs $4, and nothing fundamental has changed about the apple – it's the same quality, the same taste – wouldn't you be happy to buy more?

I look at the stock market the same way. When a stock or ETF I own goes down in price, and the underlying fundamentals are still strong, I see it as an opportunity to buy more at a discount.

Of course, if the fundamentals do change, that's a different story. If the company starts losing money, or the ETF's underlying index changes significantly, then it might be time to rebalance your portfolio. But I like to keep these changes to a minimum.

My approach is: "*When the facts changes, I can change my mind*".

And here's a crucial part of that research:
Before buying an ETF, it's vital that you go through its holdings, the portfolio allocation, and other key details. You need to understand what you're actually investing in.

The good news is that many new-age brokers now offer the ability to customize your own ETFs. This is a fantastic tool that allows you to fine-tune your portfolio and align it even more closely with your specific needs and preferences. So, take advantage of these resources!

By doing your homework upfront, you can build an "effortless" portfolio that you can stick with for the long haul.

My "Effortless" Income Strategy: Dividend ETFs in Action:
Let me give you a glimpse into how I use ETFs in my own portfolio. A portion of my investments is in Dividend ETFs.

Why? Because I like that consistent cash flow.

Now, I have the dividends automatically reinvested. This allows me to compound my returns over time. But I also have the flexibility to switch that off and receive the dividends as cash in my bank account if I need it.

Everyone's situation is different. You might be retired and rely on that dividend income to cover your living expenses. Or you might be like me, still in the accumulation phase, and want to reinvest those dividends for maximum growth.

The point is, Dividend ETFs can be a valuable tool for generating income, and how you use that income is up to you.

Chapter Summary:

Building an "effortless" ETF portfolio is about setting up a smart system from the start. Asset allocation is the foundation of this system, and it's far more important than trying to time the market or pick individual stocks. By understanding the basic asset classes, aligning your allocation with your personal circumstances, and using simple yet effective portfolio models, you can create a diversified portfolio that can help you achieve your financial goals.

ETFs make this process easier than ever, providing a cost-effective and convenient way to access a wide range of asset classes.

The key is to do your research upfront, invest with confidence, and stay the course for the long term.

Key Takeaway:

Asset allocation is the most important factor in long-term investment success. Understand your age, risk tolerance, and financial goals to determine your ideal asset allocation.

ETFs provide a simple and cost-effective way to build a diversified portfolio across different asset classes.
Dividend ETFs can be a valuable tool for generating income and enhancing returns.

CHAPTER 6

Beyond Stocks: Exploring Alternative ETF Investments

We've spent a good deal of time discussing stock ETFs, and for good reason. They're a cornerstone of many long-term portfolios. But, as I pointed out, even if you love a good global equity ETF, it's wise to remember that the investment world offers a variety of other compelling options. This chapter is your guide to those options—alternative ETFs.

We'll explore how these funds can enhance your portfolio in ways that go beyond what stocks alone can offer.

Why Look Beyond Stocks?

Let's get straight to the point: why should you consider investments beyond the stock market? It boils down to a simple but powerful concept: *resilience.*

Think of your portfolio as a ship sailing through different economic conditions. A ship with only one sail (stocks) might sail smoothly in calm waters, but it's vulnerable to strong winds or storms. A ship with multiple sails, each designed to catch different types of wind, is more likely to stay on course, no matter the weather.

That's what alternative investments can do for your portfolio. They can act as different sails, helping it navigate various market conditions.

Venturing into Alternatives with ETFs

The great thing is that ETFs make it easier than ever to access these alternative "sails."

Here's a look at some of the key asset classes you can explore:

- *Real Estate:* The Foundation Beneath the Economy

Imagine investing in real estate without the headaches of being a landlord—no leaky faucets, no late-night calls about broken heaters. That's the appeal of REIT ETFs.

REITs (Real Estate Investment Trusts) are companies that own or finance income-producing properties like apartment buildings, shopping malls, and offices. REIT ETFs, in turn, hold a basket of these REITs.

Why consider them? Real estate can provide a steady stream of income through dividends, and it tends to hold its value or even increase during periods of inflation. Think of it as adding a solid, tangible asset to your portfolio.

Gold: A Timeless Store of Value: Gold has been prized for centuries. In times of economic uncertainty, when other investments might be tumbling, gold often shines.

Gold ETFs offer a convenient way to invest in this precious metal. They typically track the price of gold by holding physical gold or gold futures.

Why gold? It's often seen as a safe haven, a place to park your money when other markets are volatile. It's not a magic bullet, but it can provide some peace of mind and act as a counterbalance to stocks.

Bonds: The Stabilizers: Bonds are essentially loans to governments or companies. They're generally less volatile than stocks and provide a more predictable income stream.
Bond ETFs allow you to easily diversify across a wide range of bonds. They can be a valuable tool for adding stability to your portfolio, especially as you get closer to retirement.

Commodities: The Building Blocks of the World
Commodities are raw materials like oil, natural gas, and agricultural products. They're the basic ingredients that keep the global economy running. Commodity ETFs provide access to these essential resources. They can offer a hedge against inflation, as commodity prices tend to rise when the cost of living increases.

Currencies: Global Exchange
Currency ETFs allow you to invest in the value of a single currency, or a basket of currencies. For example, you could invest in the Euro, or the Japanese Yen.

This can be used to speculate on the movement of currencies, or to hedge against changes in exchange rates.

Building a Balanced Portfolio with Alternative ETFs

The key to successful investing isn't just about picking individual investments; it's about how you combine them.

Here's a way to think about it.
Imagine you're creating a musical ensemble. You wouldn't want an orchestra with only violins, right? You'd want a mix of instruments—violins, cellos, trumpets, drums—each playing its own part to create a rich and harmonious sound.

That's how alternative ETFs work in a portfolio. They each bring their unique characteristics to the mix, creating a more balanced and resilient investment strategy.

For example, you might combine:

- A core holding of global equity ETFs for long-term growth.
- A allocation to bond ETFs for stability and income.
- A smaller allocation to REIT ETFs for real estate exposure and potential inflation protection.
- A small allocation to a gold ETF as a potential hedge against market uncertainty.

The specific percentages will depend on your individual circumstances, but the goal is to create a portfolio where different asset classes work together to achieve your financial goals.

Beyond the Basics: A Few Things to Keep in Mind

As you explore alternative ETFs, here are a few key considerations:

- Understanding What You Own: It's crucial to know what's inside any ETF you invest in. Look at the underlying holdings to ensure it aligns with your investment goals.

- Matching Your Goals: Are you seeking income, growth, or stability? Different alternative ETFs cater to different objectives. Choose the ones that best fit your needs.

- Long-Term Perspective: Alternative ETFs, like any investment, should be viewed with a long-term perspective. Don't try to time the market or chase short-term trends.

Chapter Summary:

Investing beyond stocks is about building a portfolio that can thrive in various market conditions. Alternative ETFs provide a convenient and cost-effective way to access a range of asset classes, from real estate and gold to bonds and commodities. By understanding the unique characteristics of these assets and how they can complement your stock holdings, you can create a more balanced, resilient, and "effortless" investment strategy.

Key Takeaway:

Diversifying beyond stocks is crucial for building a resilient portfolio. Alternative ETFs offer access to a range of asset classes, including real estate (REIT ETFs), gold, bonds, commodities and currencies.

Each alternative asset class has unique characteristics and can serve different purposes in a portfolio (e.g., income, stability, inflation hedge).

Understanding your risk tolerance and financial goals is essential for determining the appropriate allocation to alternative ETFs.

CHAPTER 7

Keeping it Effortless: Avoiding Common Pitfalls and Staying the Course

Now that you made it thus far, I'd assume you understand the power of ETFs, the importance of diversification, and how to build a portfolio that aligns with your goals.

But here's the thing: knowledge is only half the battle. The other half is *behavior*.

Even the best-laid plans can be derailed by our own human nature. We're emotional creatures, and those emotions can lead us to make poor investment decisions, especially when markets get volatile. This chapter is all about helping you understand those emotional pitfalls and giving you the tools and strategies to avoid them.

The Emotional Investor: A Cautionary Tale

Let me tell you a story. It's a story I've seen play out countless times, and you might even recognize parts of it in yourself.

Meet John. John is a smart, successful professional. He's read books on investing, understands the importance of diversification, and has built a solid ETF portfolio.

John is committed to long-term investing and knows that trying to time the market is a fool's game.

But then, the market takes a nosedive.

Suddenly, John's portfolio is down 20%. Fear creeps in. He starts reading news headlines about a potential recession, and his anxiety grows. He remembers his neighbor losing a lot of money in the 2008 crash.

"*Maybe I should sell,*" John thinks. "*I'll just get out now and wait until things calm down.*"

He sells his ETFs, locking in his losses.

Of course, the market eventually recovers. But John, now on the sidelines, misses out on the rebound. He watches as his friends' portfolios recover and surpass their previous highs.

Regret sets in.

"*I knew I should have stayed the course,*" John laments. "*Why did I let my emotions get the best of me?*"

John's story is a classic example of how emotions can sabotage even the most rational investor.

The Usual Suspects: Common Behavioral Biases

So, what exactly went wrong with John? He fell victim to a few common behavioral biases. These are psychological tendencies that can lead us to make irrational decisions, especially when it comes to money.

Here are some of the most common culprits:

- *Loss Aversion:* This is the tendency to feel the pain of a loss more strongly than the pleasure of an equivalent gain. For example, the pain of losing $100 feels much worse than the joy of gaining $100. This can lead us to sell our investments too quickly when they decline, as John did.

- *Fear of Missing Out (FOMO):* This is the anxiety that we're missing out on a great opportunity that others are taking advantage of. When the market is soaring, FOMO can lead us to chase hot stocks or invest in things we don't fully understand, just to avoid being left behind.

- *Herd Mentality:* This is the tendency to follow the crowd, even when the crowd is wrong. When everyone else is buying a particular stock or asset class, we feel pressure to do the same, regardless of its fundamentals or our own investment goals.

- *Confirmation Bias:* This is the tendency to seek out information that confirms our existing beliefs and ignore information that contradicts them. For example, if you believe a certain stock will go up, you might only read positive news about it and ignore any warning signs.

- Overconfidence: This is the tendency to overestimate our own abilities and knowledge. Overconfident investors may believe they can time the market or pick winning stocks, leading them to take on unnecessary risks.

Activity 1: Identify Your Biases

Before we go any further, let's get personal. Take a moment to reflect on your own investment experiences. Have you ever made an investment decision based on any of the biases listed above?

Think about a time when:

- You sold an investment because you were afraid of losing more money.
- You bought an investment because everyone else was talking about it.
- You ignored warning signs about an investment because you really wanted it to succeed.

Jot down your thoughts. Recognizing your own biases is the first step to overcoming them.

The Market Timing Temptation (and Why It's a Trap)

One of the most destructive biases, and one that ties into both loss aversion and FOMO, is the urge to time the market.

Market timing is the attempt to predict future market movements and buy low and sell high. It seems logical, right? If you could just get in before the market goes up and get out before it goes down, you'd make a fortune!

The problem is that market timing is incredibly difficult, even for the pros.

Countless studies have shown that even professional investors with access to vast amounts of data and sophisticated tools can't consistently time the market. The market is influenced by a complex interplay of factors, many of which are unpredictable.

Think about it:

- How do you predict a sudden geopolitical crisis?
- How do you know when a company will announce a groundbreaking new product?
- How do you anticipate a shift in investor sentiment?

The truth is, you can't.
And when you try to time the market, you're not only likely to fail, but you also risk missing out on the market's best days.

JPMorgan Asset Management did a study and found that if you missed just the best 10 days in the S&P 500 over a 20-year period, your returns would be cut in half. Miss the best 30 days, and your returns would be close to zero!

Market timing is a losing game. It's a seductive trap that can lead to poor decisions, missed opportunities, and a lot of stress.

The Power of Staying the Course

So, if market timing is a trap, what's the alternative?
It's simple, but not always easy: *Stay the course.*

Staying the course means sticking to your long-term investment plan, regardless of short-term market fluctuations. It means having the discipline to resist the urge to buy when the market is soaring and sell when it's crashing. It means focusing on your goals, not on the noise.

"*Effortless investing*" is, at its core, about staying the course. It's about setting up a well-diversified portfolio that aligns with your risk tolerance and financial goals, and then letting it do its job over the long term.

Practical Strategies for Staying the Course

Okay, so staying the course is important. But how do you actually do it, especially when your emotions are screaming at you to do something different? Here are some practical strategies:

- Have a Plan (and Write It Down): Before you invest a single dollar, create a written investment plan. This plan should outline your financial goals, your risk tolerance, your time horizon, and your chosen asset allocation. When the market gets volatile, you can refer back to your plan and remind yourself why you're investing in the first place.
- Automate Your Investments: One of the best ways to avoid emotional decision-making is to automate your investments. Set up automatic contributions to your investment accounts on a regular basis. This way, you're consistently buying, regardless of market conditions.
- Focus on What You Can Control: You can't control the market, but you can control your own behavior. Focus on the things you can control, such as your savings rate, your asset allocation, and your expenses.
- Limit Your Exposure to Noise: In today's 24/7 news cycle, it's easy to get bombarded with market news and opinions. But constantly checking the market and reading sensational headlines can fuel anxiety and lead to impulsive decisions. Try to limit your exposure to market noise. Consider checking your portfolio only once a month or even once a quarter.
- Remember Your Time Horizon: Investing is a long-term game. If you're saving for retirement, you have decades ahead of you. Short-term market fluctuations are just blips on the radar. Keep your eye on the prize.

Activity 2: Create Your "Stay the Course" Plan

Now, let's put these strategies into action. Take some time to create your own "Stay the Course" plan.
Your plan should include:

- Your long-term financial goals (e.g., retirement, financial independence).
- Your target asset allocation (e.g., 60% stocks, 40% bonds).
- Your rebalancing strategy (how often you'll rebalance your portfolio).
- Your contribution schedule (how often you'll contribute to your investment accounts).
- Your sources of support (who you can talk to when you're feeling anxious about the market).

Writing down your plan will make it more concrete and increase your commitment to sticking with it.

Regular Checkups: But Don't Obsess

While it's crucial to stay the course, that doesn't mean you should completely ignore your portfolio. Regular checkups are important, but the key is to do them in a way that doesn't trigger emotional decision-making.

I recommend reviewing your portfolio no more than once a quarter, or even once a year. During these reviews, you should:

- Check your asset allocation: Has your portfolio drifted significantly from your target allocation? If so, it might be time to rebalance.
- Review your expenses: Are you paying more in fees than you should be? Consider switching to lower-cost ETFs if necessary.
- Assess your progress: Are you on track to meet your financial goals? If not, you might need to adjust your savings rate or your asset allocation.

The goal of these reviews is to make sure your portfolio is still aligned with your long-term plan, not to react to short-term market movements.

The "Effortless" Investor Mindset

Ultimately, "effortless" investing is about cultivating a specific mindset. It's about:

- Accepting that you can't control the market.
- Focusing on what you can control: your savings rate, your asset allocation, and your behavior.
- Having a long-term perspective.
- Being disciplined and patient.
- Trusting in the power of diversification and compounding.

It's about building a portfolio that can weather any storm, and then having the emotional fortitude to let it do its job.

My Biggest Mistake (and What I Learned)

I'll be honest with you. Even as someone who understands all of this, I've made my share of mistakes.

Early in my investing journey, I got caught up in the hype surrounding a particular technology stock. Everyone was talking about it, and I didn't want to miss out. I ignored my own rules about diversification and invested a significant portion of my portfolio in this one stock.

You can probably guess what happened. The stock crashed, and I lost a lot of money.

That experience was a painful but valuable lesson. It taught me the importance of humility, the dangers of FOMO, and the absolute necessity of sticking to my long-term plan, no matter how tempting it is to chase short-term gains.

It also reinforced the power of the "effortless" approach. The times I've done best as an investor are when I've simply stuck to my plan, ignored the noise, and let the magic of compounding work its wonders.

Chapter Summary:

The biggest threat to your long-term investment success isn't market crashes or economic recessions; it's your own behavior.

By understanding the common behavioral biases that can derail investors, developing a disciplined approach, and staying focused on your long-term goals, you can keep your investing "effortless" and increase your chances of achieving financial freedom.

Key Takeaway:

Recognize and resist behavioral biases: Understand how emotions like fear and greed can lead to poor investment decisions.

Prioritize long-term goals over short-term noise: Focus on your financial objectives and avoid reacting to market fluctuations.

Create and follow a plan: Develop a written investment strategy and stick to it, even during market volatility.

Automate and limit portfolio check-ins: Set up automatic investments and review your portfolio infrequently to minimize emotional decision-making.

CHAPTER 8

Conclusion: Your Journey to Effortless Investing

Hey everyone, we've made it to the finish line! And I want to say, I'm genuinely excited for you. You're now equipped with a way of thinking about investing that can truly change your financial future.

This isn't just about picking the right ETFs; it's about something bigger. It's about taking control of your financial life in a way that's both smart and sustainable. Remember Michael, from the intro? Our "Mr. Shortcut," always chasing the next big thing? This book is the antidote to that approach. It's about building wealth the smart way, not the hard way.

And that brings me to the title of this book: "The Effortless Investor - Outsmart Wall Street's Finest Effortlessly." Let's break that down, because it's a bold claim, right?

Why "Effortless Investor"?

It might sound like I'm promising you can get rich without doing anything. That's not it at all. "Effortless" here means something very specific: it's about setting up a system that works for you, automatically and consistently, so you don't have to constantly stress, research, and trade. It's about focusing on the big picture and avoiding the noise that Wall Street throws at you every single day.

It's about recognizing that, in the long run, less is often more.

"Outsmart Wall Street's Finest Effortlessly" - Can You Really Do That?

Now, about that subtitle. Can you really *"outsmart Wall Street's finest"* by investing in a simple, "effortless" way?

The answer, backed by a mountain of evidence, is a resounding yes.

For decades, countless studies have shown that actively managed funds, run by highly paid professionals with access to vast resources, consistently underperform simple index funds over the long term.

Let's talk about some hard data.

- S&P Dow Jones Indices: Their SPIVA reports (S&P Indices Versus Active) are a goldmine of information. These reports consistently show that the majority of actively managed funds fail to beat their benchmark indices (like the S&P 500) over various time periods (1 year, 5 years, 10 years, and even 20 years).

For example, the SPIVA U.S. Year-End 2023 report found that over the past 20 years, 83% of active large-cap funds failed to outperform the S&P 500. That's huge.

Source:
https://www.spglobal.com/spdji/en/research-insights/spiva/

Morningstar: Morningstar's research also paints a similar picture. Their long-term performance data indicates that active managers struggle to keep up with their benchmarks, especially after accounting for fees.

Source: (You can find Morningstar's research and reports on their website: https://www.morningstar.com/)

These aren't isolated findings. Study after study, across different markets and time periods, confirms the same thing: the vast majority of professional money managers can't beat the market.

Why is this? There are several reasons:

- Fees: Active managers charge higher fees to cover their research and trading costs. These fees eat into your returns.
- Trading Costs: Active managers trade more frequently, leading to higher transaction costs.
- Market Efficiency: The market is incredibly efficient. Information is quickly reflected in stock prices, making it very difficult to consistently find undervalued stocks.

- Behavioral Biases: Even professionals are susceptible to the same behavioral biases that affect individual investors, leading to poor decisions.

The Power of Simplicity: Index Investing in Action

So, what's the alternative? *Index investing.*

Here's what it means in plain English:

- What is an "*Index*"? An index is like a yardstick that measures the performance of a particular market or segment of the market. The S&P 500, for example, tracks the performance of the 500 largest companies in the United States.
- What is an "Index Fund" (or ETF)? An index fund or ETF is a type of investment that aims to match the performance of a specific index. So, an S&P 500 ETF simply invests in all 500 companies in the S&P 500, in the same proportion as the index.

It's that simple. You're not trying to pick winning stocks. You're not trying to time the market. You're just buying a little piece of everything.

And guess what?

Over the long term, this simple strategy has proven to be incredibly effective.

Let me give you a real-world example. Imagine you had invested in a simple S&P 500 ETF, like the SPDR S&P 500 ETF Trust (SPY), 20 years ago. Without doing any research, without making any trades, without paying any high fees, you would have achieved a very respectable return, historically averaging around 10% per year.

I know it sounds almost too good to be true. My friend, Mr. Shortcut, couldn't believe it either. He was paying a financial advisor a 1% fee to manage his money, and they were getting him a measly 4% return. I told him, "Dude, you're basically paying them to lose money for you!"

I showed him the historical performance of the S&P 500. I explained how easy it is to buy an S&P 500 ETF. I walked him through the process of opening a brokerage account (which, by the way, is incredibly easy these days).

At first, he was skeptical. He thought investing was some complex, mysterious thing that only experts could understand. But then he saw the data. He saw how consistently a simple index fund could deliver solid returns.

He finally got it. He fired his financial advisor and started investing in low-cost ETFs. He's now on the path to building real wealth, and he's amazed at how easy it is.

That's the power of "effortless" investing. It's not about being a genius; it's about being smart enough to recognize that the market, over the long term, tends to go up, and the best way to capture that growth is to simply own a little bit of everything.

You Can Do This

I know that for many people, the stock market seems intimidating. It seems like a complex world filled with jargon and risk. But I'm here to tell you that it doesn't have to be.

You can do this. You can take control of your financial future. You can build wealth without spending hours researching stocks or worrying about every market fluctuation.

"*Effortless*" investing is about empowering you to do just that.

We've covered a lot in this book, from the basics of ETFs to building diversified portfolios to avoiding common pitfalls. You now have the knowledge and the tools to succeed.

Your Next Steps

So, what should you do now?

- Open a brokerage account: If you haven't already, open a low-cost brokerage account. The process is straightforward and can be done online in minutes.

- Choose your ETFs: Select a few broad market ETFs that align with your risk tolerance and financial goals.

- Set up automatic contributions: Automate your investments to ensure you're consistently investing, regardless of market conditions.

- Stay the course: Remember that investing is a long-term journey. Don't get discouraged by short-term market fluctuations. Stick to your plan, and let the power of compounding work its magic.

And with that, you're well on your way to becoming an *effortless investor*.

The principles and strategies you've learned in this book provide a solid foundation for building and maintaining a successful, long-term investment portfolio.

Thank you for taking this journey with me. Now, go out there and make it happen!

Dearest Readers,

I wanted to take a moment to personally thank you for reading "The Effortless Investor."

I sincerely hope this book has shown you that building wealth doesn't have to be complicated or stressful. It's really about setting up a smart system and having it work for you.

My passion for helping people achieve financial freedom led me to write my first book, "The Game of Percentage: A Simple Guide to Actually Grow Your Money." It has been incredibly rewarding to see the positive response from readers around the world. To find my book, you can search for "The Game of Percentage by Sriram Saravanan" or "books by Sriram Saravanan" or simply "Sriram Saravanan" on platforms like Amazon, Kindle, GoodReads, and Google.

I'd love to connect with you beyond the pages of this book. You may follow my Author page on Instagram "Author_Sriram_Saravanan" and can also find me on LinkedIn for professional updates and insights, www.Linkedin.com/in/SriramSaravanan

I'm also active on other social media channels where I share updates on my author journey, new book releases, and additional insights on investing. In my Blossom profile (available in the US and Canada), you can even see my portfolio and allocation. Just search for my name on Google to find me.

I'm always thrilled to hear from readers. If you've enjoyed "The Effortless Investor" or "The Game of Percentage," I'd be grateful if you could:

- Post a photo of yourself reading the book on social media and tag me!
- Share your thoughts in a review on Amazon, Google, or Goodreads. Let me know what you learned, what resonated with you, and how you plan to use the "effortless" investing approach.

Your feedback is invaluable and helps me create resources that empower you on your financial journey. I look forward to connecting and continuing this conversation with you.

Here's to your success!

Sincerely,

Sriram Saravanan

ABOUT THE AUTHOR

Sriram Saravanan is a dynamic author, and a seasoned marketer with a passion for guiding individuals on their path to financial independence.

He holds an MBA from De Montfort University in the United Kingdom, which has equipped him with the strategic insights and business acumen that define his professional and financial approach.

His debut book, "The Game of Percentage", has garnered widespread acclaim for its insightful take on beating inflation and growing wealth in real terms. Inspired by the wisdom of seasoned investors, Sriram is a firm advocate of long-term investment strategies.

Beyond his professional accomplishments, Sriram's life is enriched by his global travels. Having visited over 16 countries—including the UK, Canada, UAE, Italy, Netherlands, and more—he draws from diverse cultural experiences that add depth and richness to his work. His travels have provided him with a broader perspective on global markets, economies, and life itself, all of which influence his writing and philosophy.

Currently based in Toronto, Canada, Sriram brings a unique combination of marketing expertise, real-world financial insight, and international experience to his writing, making him a trusted voice for readers seeking practical investment advice and broader economic perspectives.

Connect with him on LinkedIn & GoodReads ***@Sriram Saravanan.***

www.ingramcontent.com/pod-product-compliance
Lightning Source LLC
LaVergne TN
LVHW090421210926
848480LV00002B/642